A Month with Mary

A PROFOUND REFORM OF HEART
IN THE SCHOOL OF MARY

BY

DON DOLINDO RUOTOLO

TRANSLATED BY

MSGR. ARTHUR BURTON CALKINS

ACADEMY OF THE IMMACULATE
NEW BEDFORD, MA
2006

A Month with Mary, A Profound Reform of Heart in the School of Mary, is a book prepared for publication by the Academy of the Immaculate [academyoftheimmaculate.com], POB 3003, New Bedford, MA 02741-3003.

© Franciscans of the Immaculate 2006
   All Rights reserved

Cum Permissu Superiorum

ISBN: 1-60114-032-0

FOR JUST ONE SOUL

The priest Dolindo Ruotolo was born in Naples on 6 October 1882 and died there on 19 November 1970 in the odor of sanctity.

His life was a drama of love for God and of suffering lived entirely in the shadow of the cross.

He was a miracle of apostolic works which consumed his strength in charity up to his last day on earth.

The spirit of penance and profound humility rendered his soul transparent to the point of concentrating all of the light of the Lord, which was shed on souls like the sun through a clear crystal ...

He wrote a commentary on the entire Old and New Testaments, 33 volumes constituting a massive and solid structure, requested by priests and laity from every part of the world. He wrote pages and pages of ascetic and mystical theology.

They called him a genius; he felt himself to be a "nothing" in the hands of God. Others didn't understand him; he responded by loving them, as only the saints know how to love.

His complete love for God and Our Lady, his fidelity to the Church, which he lived as martyrdom, were distilled in an immense love for souls for whom his prayers and sacrifices knew no limits. Even in the last years of his life (paralysis brought him to physical deterioration in ten years), even to his last days he never denied his spiritual help to souls.

How many times he was already in bed, exhausted by illnesses and overcome by weariness ... but if someone knocked at his door in the late evening to seek his help, he never allowed him to be sent away, but received him in any case! How many times he had just seated himself at his poor family table to eat his meager and penitential fare and they knocked at the door to speak with him. Immediately he rose from the table; there was a soul who was asking for help and one couldn't let him wait.

The poor meal was skipped ...

* * *

This little book, *A Month with Mary*, also originated from an act of charity of Father Dolindo.

Laura de Rosis, a person from Rossano Calabro, asked him for spiritual thoughts for every day of the month of May. The good Father Dolindo wrote thirty-one meditations for her, one for every day of the month. It was thus: everything for every soul, and his charity didn't

For Just One Soul

make it seem exaggerated for him to write a "A Month with Mary" for just one soul!

Besides, already in 1902, when he was still a theology student, he had written for his sister Maria no less than five *Dialogues of the Soul with Jesus* in a pocket sized notebook totaling 81 pages (printed in *Epistolario* 3:416–459); and from 9 to 12 October 1911 he had preached a course of spiritual exercises at the bed of the ailing Giulia Romeo of Rossano Calabro (printed in *Epistolario* 2:515–536).

Father Dolindo wrote *A Month with Mary* on pocket-sized pages joined into small fascicles of 8 to 12 pages. He sent them to Laura de Rosis every two to three days and later transcribed them with some modifications in volume III of his *Autobiography: The Story of My Life in the Plan of the Great Mercy of God*, pp. 1140 ff (cf. *Epistolario* 1:212n, 218n).

This work is from 1912: one of those years which passed in the life of Father Dolindo with the cadence of a "Way of the Cross" ... But he, serene as ever, loved Christ the more, loved Our Lady the more and reflected this love in these few pages to which he wished to give the significant title: *A Profound Reform of Heart in the School of Mary*.

A Month with Mary

These meditations are written in the style of the *Imitation of Christ*.

Meditations for just one soul!

May these pages now reach every soul who reads them as an entirely personal word, a comfort from Heaven and a portent of holiness.

First Day – Introduction
My Heart, a Flower which Mary must Cultivate

The month of Mary is the month of *a profound reform of heart*: we must leave ourselves and adorn ourselves with every virtue and every spiritual good.

In the springtime plants are reborn to a new life; they are adorned with flowers full of perfume and captivating. My soul also needs to reflower in order to be full of virtue and peace!

In your Heart, O Mary, I will reflower as a lily because you are purity. In your love my coldness will be transformed into warmth because you are full of the flames of divine charity. In your hands I will find refuge because you are the Mother of mercy!

O Mary, O Mary, cast the glance of your goodness upon me! Even I am a little flower of heaven's field ... Cultivate me and speak to me, O Mary, because by your word I will draw life and love.

MARY: O my daughter, your mother is always ready to cultivate you provided that you treat me as a mother and not as a stranger. How many times you've been afraid of me, even while knowing that I am all loving! How many times have you virtually fled from me, so slack has your devotion been. Come to my heart and let it be a school of virtue for you since God himself has made me great for your good. Follow me faithfully, even if your soul feels arid and without any fervor. Confide your pains to me. Turn toward me because in this month I have so many treasures of grace to dispense and I give them to those who turn to my motherly heart with trust.

THE SOUL: O my good Mama, don't you see what an ugly flower I am? I'm a withered flower, almost without leaves and without life. ... Help me! I entrust my soul to you that you might cultivate it and heal it. ...

The bells of your temple are ringing for the feast, Mary, yet I groan with sluggishness. Your throne is rich with flowers, and my heart, which ought to be your throne, is so poor and devoid of everything!

O my Mother, while the plaintive harmony of these bells dissipates in the air, the groan of my poor heart reaches your Heart and moves it to have pity on me! I need grace because I am so miserable: *"Maria mater gratiæ, mater misericordiæ tu nos ab hoste protege et mortis hora suscipe"*

Daily Meditations

(Mary, mother of grace, mother of mercy, protect us from the evil one and receive us at the hour of death).

ASPIRATION: O Mary conceived without sin, pray for us who have recourse to Thee.

LITTLE WORK: Accept with patience and calm the rudeness which comes your way.

Second Day
My Heart and the Heart of Mary

MARY: My little daughter, your mother is calling you and showing you what distinguishes her as Mother: *the Heart*! Draw near to my Heart, kiss it, and experience how burning is its love for you! God has submerged his mercies in it and wants it to be the center of regeneration for those children whom he has entrusted to me. You are my daughter and so entrust yourself to the Heart of your Mother who loves you so much.

THE SOUL: If you show me your Heart, Mary, I will also show you mine! How much smallness there is in my little heart! You are immaculate and pure, the delight of God and I am full of imperfections and faults! You love God immensely and I am so cold toward Him! You are so full of gifts and graces and I am your little poor one! ... O my Mother, I place my heart in yours; work on it; lift it up into the holy love of God ... reform it! It's so ugly ... even if I don't really know it yet because I'm so blinded by pride ... Tear the secrets from this heart; curtail its self-deceptions with your light; adorn it with virtues by the help of your grace so that I can truly call myself your child.

MARY: If you want to know your heart, measure it against mine. Don't believe that all is evil within you nor that all is good. Don't be discouraged or presumptuous, but recognize your weaknesses with filial simplicity without hiding them from your sight and without getting irritated ... Always remain in peace and I will help you to reform yourself.

ASPIRATION: O Heart of Mary, be my model and the refuge of my poor heart.

LITTLE WORK: Deprive yourself of something superfluous to which you feel attached.

Third Day
My Temperament

THE SOUL: *In order to reform my heart* I must study it intimately as it is, my good Mother. I look at it and I seem to see there a mass of confusion which doesn't allow me to see it clearly. How full of darkness I am! You tell me that my temperament is the fundamental character of my heart.

MARY: The temperament is the sum of the constant tendencies of the heart which propel it to act in the same way. You know your temperament from the defects into which you most often fall, from the spontaneous acts of your heart, from your habits ...

Are you very easily given to anger, ... do you get disturbed over nothing, do you react, show yourself offended? ... Are you closed, taciturn, leaden; do you build so many castles in the air? ... Are you insensitive, hard, egotistical, obstinate in your judgments? ... Are you lazy, indolent, slow, negligent, pessimistic? ... Do you see everything black and think that everyone is against you? Do you give too much weight to a word that innocently escapes from another and construe it to be an insinuation, an injury, a resentment? Do you easily hold a grudge, show resentment in small ways, react violently, backbite, grumble and even lie and calumniate? ... Are you proud, full of yourself, vain, desirous of being admired, praised, given special consideration? ... Are you greedy, attached to earthly things? Are you always looking for entertainment, ruminating about worldly ideals, hankering after your satisfactions, seeking after your tastes, complaining about your food, drink and clothing? ... Examine yourself and where you perceive major lacks there you will discover your temperament and there is the field where you must exert more effort. It isn't difficult to amend your ways; start a little at a time; begin to conquer yourself at least a few times every day and you will see that your temperament will be modified and your heart will be changed.

ASPIRATION: O Mary, deliver me from the wretchedness of my character ... from anger, from impatience ...

LITTLE WORK: If it seems that a person who has offended you deserves to be reproved, don't do it when you are still in a fit of anger, but wait until tomorrow to correct him.

Fourth Day
Imagination

MARY: Why do so many hearts that desire perfection rarely attain their objective? How many persons close themselves in silence, abandon the world, seek to free themselves from all that binds the impulses of their heart ... and yet they're always the same!

Look at a shrub covered with ivy. How beautiful it seems! The woody part is completely hidden, its leaves seem to be like a head of hair on a green trunk. ... That plant doesn't bear fruit, however; it doesn't grow; it always remains sterile ... why?

The leaves which adorn its trunk are only a parasite. The ivy beautifies the shrub externally, but it also sucks its vital forces and impedes its life. It is necessary that the trunk appears as what it is, namely a trunk, and that the leaves not be the sterile appearance of a plant, but that they be full of flowers and fruit.

How many times you also would like to appear beautiful to your own glance ... Your imagination deceives you and you cover your trunk with parasites which seemingly adorn you, but in fact take away your life.

A forced and oppressive silence is nothing other than ivy ... You are externally silent, but speak all the more internally with your imagination, with outbursts of temper, with so many castles in the air ... Get rid of this ivy! If you must converse, do it with great simplicity and preserve your heart recollected in God. Don't dream of doing harsh penances when your heart isn't yet penitent. Don't be negligent and sloppy about your clothing, but be modest and simple. Don't disguise your egotism with the tinsel of piety, but be charitable and good to all.

I want from you a gentle, sincere, profound, simple virtue, without ostentation, without vanity, without exaggeration ... So many times you dream of martyrdom when you are not capable of benefiting from the daily contrariness which you find in your family!

THE SOUL: O my good Mother, how many miseries do you not make me discover in my heart? It's true, I'm so fanciful that I believe myself to be immediately a saint, when I'm so poor in virtues ... Give me a little humility so that the parasites don't attach themselves to the humble and hidden little plants, but to the high trunks ... Make my poor heart simple so that I may live only for God.

ASPIRATION: O Mary, free my heart from false virtue. O Jesus, forgive the sins that I don't see in myself!

LITTLE WORK: If you want to do an act of virtue and realize that it would make you pleasing in the eyes of others, put off doing it to another time, if possible, when no one will see you and praise you.

Fifth Day
Hiddenness

MARY: Do you know what is the real cause of the life and the beauty of a flower? ... You see its brilliant shades, smell its delicate fragrance and yet you don't recognize that all of this buds forth from those humble roots which are hidden in the barren and often muddy earth. It is the humble earth that secures the vital part of a flower and in it that the roots are hidden and these cannot give life to the flower if they are not hidden! Virtue is always born from an intimate and profound hiddenness! Flowers must certainly be seen for Jesus says: "Let your good deeds be seen by others," but the seeds from which they bud, the *life of the heart*, must remain concealed and hidden.

How many times do you not love to appear virtuous before those who see you and seek the vain praise of others? Then you remove the root from being hidden; it unhappily dries up and the flower also wilts and dies. The paid gardener cuts the flower and ties it to an artificial stem so that it may be admired ... but in doing this he kills it! When you seek human praise, you cut the flower of virtue and you place it on an artificial stem ... After empty praise it is nothing more than a mass of withered leaves. Therefore love hiddenness and desire that only God sees you and reads the secret of your heart.

THE SOUL: O Mary, open your humble Heart to me as a refuge so that I may hide myself in it! Human praise disturbs me, agitates me, makes me so ugly and I recognize that I get worse after praise. I'm full of pride and I can't free myself of it except by hiding myself in God! O Mary, give me the strength to flee human praise and my vanity!

ASPIRATION: O Mary, give me humility of heart.

LITTLE WORK: When something redounds to your praise, don't say it for the love of holy humility.

Sixth Day
Trust

MARY: You must hide yourself in God; but precisely in order to do this, you must trust in him alone. God must be the true life of your soul, the profound peace of your heart. Hiding oneself doesn't mean being despondent; hiddenness is true when it is trusting. Often you see nothing around yourself but duplicity and deception; you see the insufficiency of the help of others, the poverty of your powers, your weakness ...

Trust, trust, and, as a fragile little child, throw yourself into the arms of your heavenly Father, who is your life, your riches, your peace! You must be hidden *in God*; you must please him alone; you must rest on him alone!

Trust in him: he looks on your faults with pity and forgives, if you repent of them with trust in his mercy. He eliminates your miseries if you offer yourself entirely to him. He comforts and sustains you in your battles, if you lean on him.

THE SOUL: I'm almost ashamed to speak with you, Mary, so far am I from this trust! Up to now I have trusted only in creatures, in my powers, in the good will of the great ones of the earth and for this I loved to make myself noticed, admired and praised. What a sad experience I've had with creatures! What a sad experience I've had with myself! Therefore I beg you to hide me in God and to help me to trust in him alone.

ASPIRATION: O Mary, my hope, expand the trust in God in my heart.

LITTLE WORK: When an act of virtue seems difficult, trust in God, and, filled with this trust, do it promptly ... Go, thus, and perform an act of courtesy for the person you find most disagreeable.

Seventh Day
God

MARY: If you are to have trust in God and hide yourself in him alone, you must meditate on him. His infinite greatness could oppress you, even while it ought to be the most beautiful subject of your trust.

What is God? He is the most pure and most perfect spirit, the Creator and Master of all things.

He is a spirit; he, therefore, being infinite, embraces all, understands all, without even minimally having to work or force himself to embrace all. Nothing escapes from the tenderness of his providence: he cares for the atom as for the giant, forgives evil, exalts virtue; he loves, he loves and is infinitely good! Such is his infinite goodness that he despises no creature. He loves all of them as a father; he regards all with pity; he watches over them, welcomes, favors them ... And if he cares with such love for all creatures, how much more does he care for you, made in his image and likeness? You see him as the great God, and yet *there is no moment when he does not stoop down to you*; you even live, move and are in him!

"How lovable you are, O my God! Even I am your creature ... you loved me even before the ages ... I was nothing and already your goodness was raising me up in your eternal designs! From the kiss of your heart I came forth pure and immaculate ... from your mercy I attained the strength to conquer the infernal enemy ... I am Mary because you are the God of infinite goodness! If you were not God, you would not have lifted me up with such goodness and mercy!"

Your mother, my daughter, is for you the living proof of that divine greatness which is infinite, yes, but is also the loving refuge for the smallest creatures! Hide yourself, then, in the heart of your God ... don't worry about the little things of this world. LOVE GOD!

THE SOUL: How can you wish that I experience no sense of bewilderment before a God so beautiful, so holy, so good, whom I have so often offended? Obtain for me, then, the pardon of my so many faults and show me that same mercy, you who are the Mother of mercy. Into your hands I entrust my soul; clothe me with yourself; present me to God because only with you my trust becomes great, in spite of my so many sins.

ASPIRATION: O my God, I thank you that you created me and that you are always near me.

LITTLE WORK: Think often during the day of the great blessedness of your soul in living under the glance of God and offer him an act of love.

Eighth Day
Jesus

MARY: I present Jesus to you this morning; he is my Son and he is the Son of God! He is the flower, the admirable, the prince of peace! Let your glance meet with his, ... and tell me if he is beautiful, if he is lovable! ... Do you not see Jesus? Jesus is Jesus because no beauty equals his, no love can describe him outside of his own love! ... Kiss this divine Heart, daughter; I give it to you so that you may love him, so that you may love him in greater depth! ...

Rest on this adored Heart ... I give it to you so that it may appease your misery, so that it may eliminate it! Submerge yourself in this sea of mercies; I present it to you so that it may cancel your fearfulness and render you full of courage, with him. Do you not see Jesus? He is your divine gardener; it is he who loves you, who lovingly cares for you, who forgives you.

Do you not hear how many words of love that he makes you hear from that Heart?

You have contemplated him disfigured, dripping with blood, full of bitterness ... has he not undergone this for your love?

You have admired him glorious and triumphant outside of the tomb ... did he not triumph in order to be your resurrection and life?

Jesus, Jesus ... is your spouse! He binds you with bonds of love that can never be broken; he has offered you to his Father as *part of his Heart* ... do you not love your Jesus?

THE SOUL: O Mary, the very name of Jesus makes me melt with love ... O how gentle and mild you are, O lovable Heart of Jesus! My fearfulness cannot endure before you because you are goodness ... O how I love you, Jesus! You are the God-man who became man for my love and precisely to stoop all the way down to me and to save me!

Therefore expand your wounds, O Jesus; I want to heal my miseries in them! Open to me your divine Heart; I want to obtain from you love and virtue! I love you, O good Jesus, I love you and you gaze on me with eyes of mercy!

O Mary, teach this poor heart of mine unlimited trust, total abandonment to a God so good! ...

Jesus! how sweet your name is, how gentle is your love, how great is your mercy!

ASPIRATION: O Jesus, I offer you my heart and my life; my Jesus, mercy!

LITTLE WORK: Call upon the holy name of Jesus during the day and for the sake of his love deprive yourself of something you really like at table.

Ninth Day
My Soul

THE SOUL: I must not only know God in order to love him, I must also know myself. The careful examination of my misery makes me annihilate myself in the sight of God and makes his compassionate mercy lower itself even to me. O Lord, how wretched I am! I'm always seeking myself, full of egotism, following my whims, full of defects and strange traits ... I find myself worm ridden and I am ashamed. Tell me, Mary, my extreme wretchedness doesn't obstruct the path of God's goodness to me, does it?

MARY: Your misery does not separate you from the mercy of God when you recognize it and humble yourself: *He never disdains a heart contrite and humbled*! God even takes delight in his poor creature when it lifts its heart up to him and sheds tears full of confidence and love at his feet. Do not fear. Embrace the cross which you have; rest yourself on my motherly Heart, which is full of love and mercy, and never let yourself worry when you perceive your misery, but lift your voice to me so that I may present you before the throne of God!

THE SOUL: ... *Myself*; here is the most treacherous enemy which I have! It is a hidden enemy because it seldom comes out in the open; it is a dangerous enemy because it lives with me and because I naturally resist fighting against it; it is an astute enemy because it deceives me with false illusions of good.

O Mary, is it not true that I always seek to excuse all of my wretchedness? ... I get easily upset if someone points out one of my flaws; I seek praise and am pleased with it; I consider others worse than me when in reality no one is worse than me. I criticize; I react in anger ... I am a heap of faults ... and yet I can hardly recognize the nothing that I am, so great is my pride!

I beg you, O Mary, to have pity on me and to teach me a little of that holy humility which made you so great so that I may recognize myself for what I am and humble myself profoundly before God. Amen.

ASPIRATION: O Jesus, deliver my soul from the delusions of evil.

LITTLE WORK: Deprive yourself of something at table.

Tenth Day
The Grace of God

MARY: The mercy of God never abandons you, little creature; it has a way of overcoming your wretchedness and encompasses you with grace.

Grace is a supernatural gift of God with which he penetrates hearts, renews them, elevates them, transforms them into himself. What water is to the arid earth grace is for your heart. The Holy Spirit, who is the substantial love of the Father and the Son, consumes your misery with his gifts if only you cast it into those divine flames and thus he transforms you into a new being.

Grace is the support of human freedom because it is its guide, its help, its lifting up ... Your soul is well established when it is under the influence of this divine grace.

Do you feel drowsy in your spirit? Lift your eyes up to God; call upon the Holy Spirit and beg him to awaken you to life and to divine love.

Do you feel depressed and disheartened? Call upon this infinite love in order to be lifted up; thus you will become accustomed to live in a spirit of continual offering and you will touch with your hand what is impossible to you, but very possible to the grace of God!

You see me so rich and great. You are astounded at this, yet all of this greatness was the work of the grace of God; you say this to me yourself in your greeting: *Hail Mary, full of grace.*

The grace of God is not frugal or stingy because *it is the expansion of love.*

You must, therefore, distrust yourself and trust much in the grace of God ... Come to me, little flower of Jesus; I will rearrange your little leaves, I will revive you, I will immerse you in the mercy of Jesus. God has made me the channel of that grace which must enrich and enliven you.

ASPIRATION: Mary, Mother of grace, have pity on me.

LITTLE WORK: Recite five Hail Marys to beg a treasure of graces from the Heart of Mary.

Eleventh Day
Mary's Grace

THE SOUL: Hail, O Mary, full of grace! ... From the wretched earth where I am, I raise up my glance to you to admire you and I see you resplendent, beautiful, clothed in glory ... Hail, O Full of grace! How the little things of this world seem vile next to you who by grace have reached the highest summits of perfection ... Hail, Mother of God, my Mother! You are *the most beautiful work of the Lord's hands*, you are a *monument of divine mercy*, you are the *glory of his love* ... Hail, O Spouse of God!

You are the creature who loved God so much, who overcame the poverty of human nature, and flew directly to the Infinite without ever deviating. The grace of God lent you these wings of love and you were pure, immaculate, all-beautiful, all-holy ... Hail, O Mary!

I admire you, O Mother; the Angels pay homage to you and exalt you; the human generations call you "blessed" and raise up monuments of thanks and love to you ... you are the all-holy ... Hail, O Mary!

Oh! Who could have imagined that a flower so beautiful could be born of the pitiable stock of Adam? ... You entered into this world full of grace: Hail, O Mary! I am small, but I am happy because I am your child. You look after me, you guide me, you lift me up. In you I have found support and life because you are the inexhaustible channel of divine mercies: Hail, O Mary!

Hail, O Mary; your sweet glance lifts me up and makes me live because your glance is full of mercy! Take my soul into your heart as a little flower and, if instead of finding fragrance, you find parasites, cleanse it with your hand full of goodness.

Hail, O Mary! You are my life, my sweetness, my hope, O full of grace, O Immaculate Virgin. Amen.

ASPIRATION: O Mary, my hope, to you I entrust my soul.

LITTLE WORK: Abstain during the day from innocent acts of curiosity.

Twelfth Day
The Channels of Grace

MARY: In his mercy God did not want to make the flow of his grace to you difficult and he gave you a channel through which you can enrich yourself with it in the holy sacraments.

A sacrament is a sensible sign, instituted by Jesus Christ, through which grace is conferred. These sensible signs are like titles that give you a true right to the grace of God since he instituted them for this specific purpose. What treasure there is in the holy sacraments! How shortened the way of perfection remains because of them and how easily one attains to God!

Among the works of piety, always give the first place to the sacraments because the other works *can* yield the fruit of grace and mercy, while the sacraments *certainly do so*, being grounded on the merits of Jesus Christ.

You always complain about your spiritual weakness and yet you have in hand the most secure means to be purified and strengthened.

A Month with Mary

Without the sacraments the soul is abandoned to itself and cannot live the higher life which, you realize, flows from the Heart of Jesus.

THE SOUL: How many times, O Mary, have I not been lost in delusions of a false and superficial piety? I've been careless in receiving the holy sacraments because I haven't appreciated their value. Confession and Holy Communion have become for me a rather bothersome routine while I have given myself to the caprice of so many sterile and empty practices of piety in which I sought my tastes and my satisfaction. I repent bitterly for having lost so much time and for having reduced myself to being like a barren fig tree, full of leaves, but without fruit.

You, who are the Mother of mercy and channel of every grace, obtain for me from Jesus forgiveness for so much ingratitude and the grace to appreciate the holy sacraments. Make me docile to grace when I receive them so that, like a humble little plant sprouting at the foot of the Cross, I may receive the vital fluid which flows from the Heart of Jesus.

ASPIRATION: O Jesus, give me the grace to receive the sacraments well in life and at the hour of my death.

LITTLE WORK: If you experience repugnance at performing some service at home, master yourself for the love of God without complaining and without showing others your discomfort.

Thirteenth Day
Holy Baptism

MARY: The grace of God has enriched you from your birth. You came into the light crying. You were very tiny, but your soul had need of God. A humanly insurmountable barrier was interposed between you and God. You were a slave of the original fault. You were born with the curse that the first man passed on to you as a sad inheritance. This original fault deprived you of a great good: friendship and familiarity with God.

The Lord gave you back a new life, incorporating you into Jesus Christ, you, a creature of Adam, became a creature of the Redeemer, a child of the new Adam from whom you inherited the blessing.

The saving water of Baptism descended on your forehead ... the heavens opened, the kiss of God's mercy renewed you; you were thus purified and emerged holy and innocent because you found yourself united to Jesus the Redeemer, who with his Blood had washed away all sin. How many angels came around your crib to contemplate the sublime beauty of your soul made innocent and a little child of God!

Daily Meditations

Always remember with gratitude that grace which God conferred on you. You will be able to gauge it only in eternity.

With Baptism Jesus incorporated you into himself, but preserved intact your freedom and your state of being an exile and a pilgrim. For that reason you made *promises* to the Lord that were like the *consecration of your freedom to God*.

With Baptism you were elevated to a superior state and thus you renounced all that is low and vile that the world gathers together or offers as pasturage to your lower nature, and the demon. You renounced the world, the flesh and the devil and offered yourself to God, to the Redeemer and to the Holy Spirit whose living temple you became.

When you feel pulled toward the earth and hear the suggestions of the world, of the flesh and of the devil, remember your promises and do not further desecrate the grace of Baptism. Remember that you are a Christian and you must not dishonor this Baptismal character with a materialistic and disordered life.

Because you are incorporated into Jesus Christ, you must glorify him in your life and being as his fragrance.

THE SOUL: O my Mother, how many bitter tears should I shed at the remembrance of my Baptism! I was beautiful and innocent; I was dear to God and yet I have degraded myself with so many sins! Lift up the weakness that so many wounds have caused and grant that I may wash away my sins with the tears of the most lively sorrow! How many times have I been ashamed even of being Christian and have lived completely immersed in the spirit of the world! How many times have I soiled the garment of my innocence! O Immaculate Heart of Mary, receive me into yourself and have pity on this poor little flower, so often broken, so many times stripped of its leaves by the hurricane of evil.

ASPIRATION: O Mary, make me truly Christian, make me faithful to the promises made in Holy Baptism.

LITTLE WORK: Reflect that the world is a deceiver and only knows how to give bitterness even when it promises pleasures and triumphs.

Fourteenth Day
The Spirit of the World

MARY: You live in the world and you cannot withdraw yourself from it materially, but you must be there without living in its spirit. What a turbulent whirlwind is the world! It lives on egotism because it lives with a fixation on pleasure. No ideal lifts it up beyond that of the material and even when it seems to have an ideal, it seeks only itself in vainglory and applause, in other words in the sensory satisfaction of a passion. From whence is born duplicity, fraud, lies, injustice, showing off, pride, impurity ... Hence the world is like a sea during a storm, which knows no peace; he who falls into this sea feels all of the cold of its waves and is knocked around by its swirling motion until it gets smashed against the reefs of sin!

Everything in the world is vile and full of anguish; everything degrades man and makes him a slave, drying up in him the most beautiful life which is the life of the soul: fashions, make-up, vanity, infatuations, entertainments are thorns that prick and miseries that degrade! Here is the one whom you renounced in Baptism. Does it not seem to you a great grace to trample on all the rottenness of the world and to be propelled into the simplicity and peace that lead to God?

It is not a sacrifice for you to renounce the world, but a joy!

To renounce the world you don't have to enclose yourself in a hermitage; you must only be truly Christian and live as the branch united to the vine, in the intimacy of union with Jesus Christ, into whom you have been incorporated by holy Baptism.

Look at the glorious army of the saints, that is to say those who have renounced the world. You will find them in every condition: there are faithful spouses, upright mothers, innocent virgins, young people who lived in the fresh innocence of their age; there are the little, the humble and also kings and the great. Look at the glory with which they are clothed …

At the same time, look from on high at the world with its lies, its delusions, its forms of slavery, its complications, its struggles and consider how it is a great good and a noble thing for you to renounce the world and to cleave to the truth and to God! … This renunciation is not a sacrifice for you; it is a grace.

ASPIRATION: O Jesus, grant that I may live in you and flee the delusions of the world.

LITTLE WORK: If you encounter some attachment in your life to the trifles of the world, to its fashions, to its vanities, break it immediately and energetically as unworthy of you who are Christian.

Fifteenth Day
The Spirit of Jesus Christ

MARY: Opposed to the spirit of the world, which is a mass of duplicity, resentment, struggles, presumption and degradation, is the spirit of Jesus Christ, who is the way, the truth and the life. Hear his word: "Learn from me for I am meek and humble of heart ... Blessed are the poor in spirit, blessed are those who weep for they shall be consoled, blessed are those who suffer persecution for justice' sake ..."

These are words which seem audacious and yet the great secret of happiness and of peace is hidden in them.

What good is it to have many riches, if they leave you always unhappy, even more, if they cause you the disquiet of always wanting more? Far more excellent it is to renounce all that is unused and superfluous and to rest in the desire of possessing God.

What good is it to dominate others with the impetuosity of your character? In reality you do not dominate, but you become the object and the target of a thousand battles which embitter the soul. Far more excellent is the

Daily Meditations

humility and the meekness which give you the possession of the hearts of men.

What good is it to laugh and amuse oneself on earth if the laughter is changed into bitter tears? Calm and resigned suffering, on the other hand, gives you freedom for the impulses of the spirit, and thus, even while weeping you are consoled. You remain truly consoled because you feel like a pilgrim on the earth; you detach yourself from what oppresses you and you experience God all the more!

What good are the pleasures of the senses? Every pleasure is changed into a thorn and you feel cast into the distressing gloom of remorse ... Far more excellent is the purity which brings you peace and allows you to gaze with clear vision into the immensity of God!

Believe in your Blessed Mother, who more than all other creatures lived in the spirit of Jesus Christ; there is nothing more beautiful, more elevated, more agreeable than to live in him. Therefore renounce your whims, your resentments, your disordered desires. Look upon all things in God and live glorifying him, aspiring to your only goal which is the heavenly fatherland.

ASPIRATION: O Jesus, meek and humble of heart, make my heart like unto thine.

LITTLE WORK: When you realize that you are lacking in meekness, perform a little service for the person whom you have displeased.

Sixteenth Day
Renouncing the Demon

THE SOUL: I know that in holy Baptism I renounced the demon and I'm happy with that renunciation. The demon is so repulsive that I really would not want to make friends with him! ...

Yet so many times I've been overcome by his suggestions and by sinning I've preferred him to God himself. How awful is my ingratitude and how revolting is my foolishness!

The demon is a degraded being, ... he is a monster, without order, without happiness, without life! In his fall he didn't lose his natural qualities, but what are they worth? They are also the greatest torment for him.

An angel is a spirit who lives by truth and admirable activities; now the demon lives by lies because he is forever far from the eternal and essential Truth; he lives without real activity, but in toilsome agitation.

No. I will never more go near his promptings and I beg your solid support, O Mary, to overcome him. You are the conqueror of the demon; you crush his head. You have been lifted up as the morning star of the world and

A Month with Mary

your Immaculate Conception represented the most splendid triumph over the demon. Widen your mantle, O Mary, receive me; defend me from the snares of the demon! You are the all-pure, the all-beautiful, the all-gentle, ... you are my mother!

Unfortunately so many times, I have made myself the slave of the demon and for this reason I now fear my weakness.

Queen of the angels, protect me, remove far from me the specter of evil, the delusions of my senses, the attractions of pride, the impulses of my corrupt nature.

Go far away from me, Satan, pasture of death, go far away from me. I enjoin this on you in the name of Mary Immaculate, who triumphantly crushed your momentary and disastrous power! Go far away from me because I already belong to my God and I have been purified by his mercy. Go far away from me; I command this of you in the name of Jesus who conquered you with his Blood! In this divine Blood I have found life again and you will no longer have dominion over me!

ASPIRATION: You are all-beautiful, O Mary, and there is no stain in you; you are my Mother.

LITTLE WORK: When you are tempted, make the sign of the Cross and call on the names of Jesus and Mary.

Seventeenth Day
The Passions and the Flesh

MARY: The demon penetrates into you by means of the passions and, if you do not deny yourself, your battle against the demon is vain and fruitless.

A passion is a disordered movement of your physical being or of your soul which makes you forget the high supernatural end to which you tend and reduces you within yourself.

It is the keen desire for relief, for comfort that you look for in the mire because mire is all you see around you when you lose sight of your ultimate end.

It is a reaction to the law of God when you don't see its beauty and harmony; it is a rebellion against God when you seek pleasure, peace and happiness outside of him. Sometimes deluding poetry dazzles you and you dream of reaching high peaks of glory and pleasure when in reality you are falling into the abyss.

Sometimes you see nothing but this present life and fail to recognize that all is passing ... then you concentrate on everything on this earth, on your material well-being and go about seeking the deceptive love of creatures, riches, comfort, applause, pleasures, amusements. The demon is waiting for you at the pass in these dark narrow straits along your way; he presents objects which attract you; he upsets you with images which get you stirred up and thus he catches you in your own snares in order to drag you into his abyss. Don't deceive yourself; combat your passions as soon as they manifest themselves and flee the occasions which make them take on giant proportions!

If you live in the world and flit around flames like an inexperienced butterfly, you will get burnt. Close your eyes to the distorted visions of your lower nature, your ears to the vain words of men, your heart to the vain affections of the senses. Nourish your soul on truth; nourish it on Jesus in the Blessed Sacrament.

It is in the eternal Truth and eternal Love that the passions drown and die.

The more you know God, the more you live by faith, the more you lift your gaze above, the more you immerse your heart in Jesus, the less you feel the weight of your flesh and the delusions of the false mirages of the passions. *Converse* with God because in him you will experience the beauty of your final end and the miserable attractions which you feel in yourself will vanish into nothingness.

ASPIRATION: O Mary, give me the grace to seek God and to delve deeply into the beauty of eternal truth.

LITTLE WORK: For the love of God, deprive yourself of some amusement which seems harmless to you. An amusement is often like the spark that ignites the fire of the passions in the heart.

Eighteenth Day
My Miseries

THE SOUL: At your feet, O Mary, I want to consider once again the miseries of my nothingness in order to appreciate better the solemn renunciation which I made in holy Baptism. My renunciation was not a concession, a gift which I made to God; rather it was a great grace which he conceded to me so that my renunciation of self is really equivalent to my liberation from all that lowers and dishonors me. With this renunciation I abandoned the mire for infinite richness and I raised myself to Jesus in order to become a living member of his body, I who was a poor cursed atom! ...

O Mary, how good Jesus has been to me and how little I have recognized and appreciated him! The sacrifices which even now he asks of me are really only the great benefits of his love!

What am I? I am a mass of miseries! God only asks me to rid myself of these miseries and to me it seems an act of generosity not to give myself to him.

What am I? While I lift myself up to God I feel a force in me that presses me down into the most vile desires.

God asks of me nothing other than to renounce this baseness.

I lose myself in so many castles in the air and in the whirlwind of my dreams. God only asks me to renounce these vain and tormenting dreams in order to breathe in reality.

The satisfactions of the flesh are so thorny ... every gratification is in reality an abyss into which I fall, in the bottom of which I then become agitated and take pleasure. God only asks me to emerge from the abyss to live in the fragrant heights of the perennial spring of life. Yet, I'm so ungrateful to the Lord that every fleeting image throws me off balance and I flee further away from him, attracted by the gauche mirages of this world!

O Mary, break these chains which still bind me to myself and to the world, and, since God looks upon the renunciation of so many miseries as an act of generosity worthy of the eternal reward, and because these attract me, make me generous with God, so that I may be less unworthy of your so many mercies.

Lord, my God, receive me as a holocaust, even though I am so miserable; *I have nothing to give up to you but my misery*, and I burn it on the altar of your divine will. You alone be my hope and my life.

ASPIRATION: O Mary, free me from ingratitude and from my miseries.

LITTLE WORK: Make an act of offering of yourself to God and resolve to renew it every day.

Nineteenth Day
Soldier of Jesus Christ

THE SOUL: I was signed with holy Chrism, O Jesus; I girded myself with a mystical sword and solemnly said: I will do combat for your glory!

It was a solemn day for me: the Bishop, vested with the holy stole, invoked the Holy Spirit upon me; he extended his hands over my head to proclaim the dominion of God over me, he anointed me with oil to consecrate me to him and to fortify me; and then he made me repeat the profession of faith in order to initiate me into the spiritual combat. I arose happy and found next to me a dear person who was committed to helping me in this battle ...

You smiled on me, O Jesus, because I felt my soul full of peace and you awaited from me an authentic and strong testimony before the lying and faithless world.

The sword which you gave me was beautiful. You signed me with the sign of the cross to tell me that *you must be my strength*, that you must be my confidence, that you must be my glory.

Daily Meditations

That cross, signed on my forehead with oil, disappeared, but it was to remain in my works, in my life, in my soul; I myself was to be like a triumphant cross, a glorious trophy of your redemption!

Thus you set me apart for yourself, I was much more yours and I confirmed at your feet the solemn promise of my Baptism, while you confirmed me in your mercy!

O how great are your sacraments, O Jesus!

How many battles I've had since I've been confirmed; I should have fought and in the meantime I've been defeated because I've rendered your so many mercies and helps vain! O Jesus, I am covered with disgrace, and here I am wounded at your feet! Please forgive me! Let the grace of the Sacrament of Confirmation be revived in me; make me strong; make me faithful to your love.

Love is the most beautiful characteristic of your soldier and for this the eternal love of God descended on me ... O Jesus, detach me from all; inflame me with your love so that, loving you, I will defend you and will not be unfaithful to you.

ASPIRATION: God the Holy Spirit, inflame me with love.

LITTLE WORK: Perform some act of zeal to repair for all of the cowardice which you've been guilty of in the divine service.

Twentieth Day
Spiritual Combat

MARY: The life of man is warfare on the earth. He, like a soldier, does not have a fixed home, but a provisional one and must go where the will of God calls him. Your first combat must be that undertaken for the defense of the faith. You will often find yourself among people who do not believe or who are so weak in the faith that they give way at the smallest obstacle, often even at the ridicule of fools. You must counter, manifesting your unlimited submission to the wisdom of God, who is the supreme and only Truth, esteeming and appreciating it above all human theories.

If you allow yourself to be carried away or vacillate when some puny scientist of the earth contradicts the eternal Truth, you are not a soldier of Jesus Christ; you are guilty of desertion. *The faith is the greatest science*; it is not blind or traditional assent to things incomprehensible, but it is the superior revelation of the highest truths which you admit because God has revealed them to you, God who deserves more faith than any scientist of the earth. Therefore you must affirm your faith against all of the snares and contrary affirmations of pathetic earthly wisdom, apostatized from God.

Affirming your faith, you must of necessity show yourself a child of the Catholic Church which possesses the sacred deposit of revealed truths; you must, therefore, fight boldly against every current that would pull you out of the Church and affirm your submission to its authority, to the pope, to the bishops, to the priests.

You must fight against distrust and show that you trust in God and adore his dispositions, conforming yourself to his divine will. One is not worthy of God who is excessively preoccupied with earthly things, who despairs, who puts his faith back in men, forgetting God. You must fight against the delusions of the world and show yourself a Christian in life; you will never follow what is opposed to the will of God; you will not follow the customs and fashions of the world, even at the cost of being mocked, even at the cost of suffering and martyrdom.

A Christian fights energetically when he lives as a Christian, when he shows himself to be living according to the law of God and of the Church, when he is zealous for the salvation of his own brothers. Life itself is the most beautiful battle and therefore your life is a warfare here on earth.

And the weapon of your spiritual combat is prayer.

Pray because you must fight not only to destroy evil, but also to spread the good; pray because in order to fight you must first conquer yourself and live totally united to God.

As a Christian you must nourish your soul with the sacraments, you must enlighten it with knowledge of and meditation on the eternal truths; you must enliven it with constant union with God, fleeing from sin as from death itself, and humbling yourself in his presence.

ASPIRATION: O Jesus, give me the grace to bear witness before men so that you will then receive me on the day of judgment.

LITTLE WORK: Repeat the act of faith at least three times during the day.

Twenty-first Day
Human Respect

MARY: Among the enemies you must fight against, my child, there is one who is small, wretched, foolish, but who can paralyze you. This enemy seems to be outside of you, but in reality is none other than yourself. Babies go near the mirror, look at themselves, get frightened at seeing a being that moves, become timid or want to play with it, but ... that being which frightens them or fascinates them is none other than their own image.

You do the same when you allow yourself to be vanquished by human respect: it seems to you that the others assault you, that they are playing tricks on you, that they persecute you, but in reality it is you who are so weak in your faith that you believe that this can manage to cause you dishonor or damage. What a shame for you, who are so ennobled by the profession of your faith, to hide it or disparage such greatness for fear of stupid and vile raillery!

When you are seized by an idea, when you believe that something will glorify you, you don't fear any jesting and, if they jeer at you, you not only reject it, you despise it.

Daily Meditations

Are you ashamed of elegant clothing because someone teases you? No, in fact you're proud of it. You show it off because you are convinced that it is refined; if you were convinced of the contrary, you would be embarrassed to go out dressed like that and it would seem to you that you were the butt of everyone's gossip. If, then, you are embarrassed to be seen as Christian, it is because in reality you are not—you don't feel it, you don't live it and your faith is like clothing that barely covers the miserable rags of the world which you haven't yet discarded!

But, tell me, isn't Jesus your glory, your life, your strength? Are you not convinced that his wisdom vanquishes all human wisdom and that his principles are truth, justice and good? So why do you fear the evil eye of the world and fraternize with it?

In reality, my child, the world laughs at false piety and false faith. Even while it fights against a Christian, the world admires him, and if it saw in you a real Christian, the world would not make fun of you. Children do not sneer at a lady who wears an elegant hat, they rather jeer at the lady who wears a hat while wearing a shabby, worn out dress. It's the same for you.

But even if the world ridicules you, what's that to you? Must the world judge you? What will you respond to the eternal Judge, if he protests that he will be ashamed of whoever is ashamed of him? So lift up your countenance from the abjection into which you have fallen. Remove all that is not Christian from your life, from your thoughts, from your practices, from your words and show before the world with deeds that you love and esteem God above all things.

ASPIRATION: O Jesus, O Jesus, you alone above all things.

LITTLE WORK: If in conversation God is offended by complaining—or worse by speaking badly of the faith, of the Pope, of priests, of one's neighbor—intervene energetically and protest or break off the conversation and move away.

Twenty-second Day
The Misery of Human Judgment

MARY: You are so afraid of human judgment and so many times you betray God in order not to contradict a poor creature. But what is man? What value has his scornful word or his threats? You fall with regard to human respect not only out of cowardice, but also because of self-interest and you dissemble or betray your faith for fear of being taken amiss by men.

But what is man? Is he perhaps the master or arbitrator of the world? Have you so little faith in the goodness and providence of God to believe that he abandons you when you endanger your own situation for love of him? How many times do you not try to win human benevolence by pretending to be without faith, impartial and free! ...

Fool! in reality you do nothing then but entrust yourself to men of the earth who are deceitful, egotists and traitors! And are you not ashamed to put yourself in such a cowardly way under the most degraded and vile men of the earth? What is man in his judgments? The history of human knowledge tells you: man despises today what he applauded yesterday; he affirms and denies, he contradicts himself, lies or feels his way along in the darkness of doubt.

Who are they who discredit your faith? They are those who do not know it; weak and cowardly souls who are ironically called strong souls; impure people who don't see the truth because their god is their belly, because they love pleasure and orgies of the passions. And you would fear the judgment of these poor unfortunates?

The wisdom of God, on the contrary, like a brilliant star, rises ever alive and immortal in the midst of men and you must fear only the judgment of God.

Don't worry about men, then; they can't do you any harm because God alone is the master of all. Fear God and trust in him with firm confidence. Do all that you are supposed to.

Even if accomplishing it should cost you your life, before you there have been millions of glorious martyrs who give you the example of the most perfect and Christian self-denial. The form of this world soon passes, illusions fall, sham human power comes tumbling down ... blessed are you if you can present yourself in the sight of God clothed in his glory, cloaked in his justice and in his charity!

ASPIRATION: O Jesus, make me appreciate your greatness and despise the world.

LITTLE WORK: Rather than fear human judgment, seek to bring back to the faith with great charity those who despise it.

Twenty-third Day
The Aspirations of the Heart

MARY: A soldier who wants to keep himself really faithful to his duty should not be one who serves under constraint; he should have an ideal toward which he aspires. In moments of danger in which it seems as if life is slipping away, in which he feels the full impact of the adversary, the soldier takes up his arms and at the outcry of his ideal, he musters all of his energy and wins.

Look at your heart for a moment, my child, and study it with regard to its supreme aspirations ...

You gaze on me, your eyes contemplate the immaculate candor of my soul and you sense all the beauty of purity.

You see me in profound recollection; in *my countenance you read the life of infinite Love which attracts me* and you want to fly, fly, like a little bird that flutters anxiously when it sees the magnificent flight of its mother! ...

You see me with downcast countenance ... desolate from the bitter grief of Calvary. Expand your heart and cry out: Mother, grant me to weep with you!

Daily Meditations

You, therefore, must aspire to innocence, to the infinite, to the sacrifice which will lead you to these two harbors of true happiness!

I saw you so many times involved in worldly affairs, but you were not happy with them and you remember now with regret. As you advance in years, you perceive in life something more elevated than what appears ... *you want God*! Nothing satisfies you; nothing consoles you; all of your castles in the air begin to crumble and collapse; you desire God! Only his charity convinces you; only his love satisfies you; only his friendship gives you peace!

Lift yourself up, then, in great purity of heart: "Blessed are the pure in heart for they shall see God." Jealously preserve the innocence which Jesus has given back to you in the Baptism of his blood when he received the tears of your repentance and purified you. Flee the frivolous company of creatures because you will not find God in the hubbub of human affairs.

Recollect yourself in your nothingness because God only stoops down to holy humility, as he lowered himself even to me, because *he looked upon me in my interior annihilation*.

Don't flee the cross; rather carry it willingly close to Jesus. It is the key to heaven; it is the door that introduces you into the kingdom of the eternal aspirations of your soul ...

The little human things will soon pass away; they will fall into oblivion ... I will garner you like a lily of the valleys to adorn the heavenly garden.

ASPIRATION: O Jesus, may your kingdom come soon!

LITTLE WORK: Avoid saying useless words in order to maintain the holy recollection of the soul.

Twenty-fourth Day
A Canticle of Love

(According to the Spirituality
of the *Canticle of Canticles*)

THE SOUL: O Jesus ... the only desire of my soul, only good of my being, come!

With the sighs of my soul I call upon you because you are the only true beauty, come!

My beloved is snow-white as a lily, ruddy as a rose ... his flowing disheveled hair attracts me ... how beautiful you are, O beloved of my soul! ... Come! ...

Everything becomes a voice that calls me to you alone because where you pass you strew a thousand allurements of love! ... You smiled upon creation and it became a delightful harmony that speaks of you ... Come!

I am an exile and pilgrim in this vale of tears, but you have shown yourself to me as my all ... come, O Jesus, yes, come!

My voice is weak, but I unite it to the concert of all creation; it becomes strong with your very merits ... come, O my Spouse!

A Month with Mary

I went wandering the ways of the world, but couldn't find you ... I asked the sentries about you ... but they only keep watch over little human miseries ... I kept walking and walking and then in the solitude of the lilies I saw you!

What a vision of love! Your clothing was snow-white; around your head there was an aureole of glory and from your lips came a word of love! ... How beautiful you are! ...

My step is slight; I sigh for you with all of the impulse of my soul, come, O Jesus! My soul loves you, it loves you ... it loves you, O infinite God because you are my only desire ... Come! ...

O don't distract me from my Beloved, O little things of the earth; you are a fatuous light and I find in you only coldness and death! It is only my Jesus that I desire ... Come, O Jesus! ...

I want love in this poor soul of mine and you alone give it to me: come, O Jesus!

I desire sufferings because through the sufferings I will love you the more. The sufferings you send are only a path of charity; come, bring me the cross, come into my soul!

I love you, O my only true good! Please don't gaze on me any more ... the heart inflames me with love and then leaves me desolate and poor! I will then love you between the delightful beatings of my heart with a disinterested love ... Come, O Jesus!

I love you, Jesus, and because I love you I desire only you!

Let the creatures torment me; they only drive me closer to you ... Among the contradictions which they will cause me, you will hear all the better the voice of my love ... Come! ...

They despise me as inept and I really am because I am nothing but misery! But to my nothingness you are a support, you are peace, you are all because you are Jesus! ... Come! ...

Jesus, my Jesus, your little creature gets disturbed, but does little; you know me well ... hence come to me and raise me up in your mercy ... Come, O Jesus! ...

Love, love, how delightful you are when you are born of that Heart of divine fire, of my Jesus! Look at me, O my Angels; Jesus has already bound me to himself ... My love, give me a kiss of mercy and of love! ...

O Jesus, you have already come ... O that I might die, then, in a cry of love ... I love you! ...

The bonds that bind us are sealed in your Blood ... you will cast me away from you no more for you are too good! ...

O Jesus, O Jesus, O my love ... you alone! ...

You are here in my heart! ... you alone! ...

You are king of my soul! ... you alone! ...

You are my peace! ... you alone! ...

You are all, O my love! ... you alone! ...

I no longer have the strength to speak ... my Love! ...

Praise God from the heavens; praise him, O Angels; praise him, all creatures; praise him, O Mary! ... God alone! ...

ASPIRATION: Long live Jesus! ... Thank you, O Jesus, who live in my soul!

LITTLE WORK: Seek pardon of the person you have most offended or who has a grudge against you so that the aversion and upset do not block love.

Twenty-fifth Day
The Eucharist

MARY: Jesus was not content merely to open to you the channels of grace with the Sacraments; he wished to give you himself so that you could live totally by him and in him. At the vigil of his sufferings he wished to leave you a perpetual reminder of love; he took some bread, broke it and gave it to his disciples saying: "Take this and eat it, this is my Body." Likewise he took the chalice with wine, blessed it and gave it to his disciples saying: "Take and drink, this is my Blood." From that moment the world possessed the greatest marvel: bread transubstantiated into his Body and wine transubstantiated into his Blood! With the Body and with the Blood are also the soul and the divinity, in such a way that when you eat of this bread of life, you receive the whole Jesus as he is now, glorious in heaven.

Jesus did not give himself to you in vain: he comes to you in order to incorporate you into himself, to give you his very life, to supply for your weakness, to sustain your soul. You should not, then, complain uselessly of being destitute of every virtue, but you must go to the banquet of life to be healed of your spiritual sicknesses.

Jesus is not upset to see you cold when he sees you humble and constant ... He is there precisely to warm your coldness. Don't put obstacles before him, but offer yourself to him totally and rest in his goodness. Certainly your Communion will not remain fruitless when you go to Jesus with at least a humiliated heart, but you cannot always be aware of the fruitfulness of your Communion.

Alas! Your miseries are so many and you do not know them, but Jesus patiently eliminates a few of them each time. You are not aware of this secret work and you would just like to be conscious of sensible fervor and thus to please yourself. Thus you believe that your Communion is without fruit and that is not true! If Jesus gave you the relish and the fervor without first rooting love in you, you would be a barren soul, a fantasy flame! ...

Entrust yourself to him, never back away from him. The more you are in his company, the sooner you will be filled with his life. Don't satisfy yourself merely with receiving him; go to visit him, prostrate yourself before his glorious throne, implore his blessing, direct your thought to him during the day, desire him spiritually in your heart, pray, pray that he may reign in you.

Daily Meditations

ASPIRATION: O Sacrament most holy, O Sacrament divine, all praise and all thanksgiving be every moment thine!

LITTLE WORK: Make a Communion of reparation for one who is far from the Holy Eucharist.

Twenty-sixth Day
The Transformation of the Soul

JESUS: "He who eats my flesh and drinks my Blood will have eternal life and I will raise him up on the last day ... He who feeds on me lives because of me ... Your fathers ate the manna and died, but he who feeds on me will not die ... I am the bread of life come down from heaven."

Here are the words with which I prepared faithful souls for the great mystery of love; here is the meaning and the nature of this great Sacrament of life. The human soul in contact with mine becomes transformed; it becomes one with me; it lives because of me. It becomes transformed not by an instantaneous miracle, but gradually and precisely in the same manner that physical life is supplied with food.

Your soul, too, my child will be transformed into me; don't be in a hurry to see yourself perfect all at once. The Eucharist does not burn sensibly; it was not instituted to give you superficial gratification, but to give you *life*. You must live from me, identify with me, abandon yourself to me and hence you must experience your emptiness, your nothingness, your inertia in profound humiliation.

Even material food is of itself effective in supplying life, even though it does not produce the same effects in all. One eats and visibly grows because the body assimilates the food well. Another eats and with the nourishment comes the strength to avoid an illness, to prevent a collapse, to expel noxious or infected germs from the organism. To these food might seem unnecessary, but it is not so.

I will change you completely, but I will not do violence to your nature; I will penetrate into you gently and virtually without making you aware. Do not tire of me ... always come to me; never stop seeking me because in me you will find life.

THE SOUL: O my Jesus, you know my misery well and you know that I am only nothingness! Here is my soul, I place it in your hands: you transform me!

Bread of life, give me the life that will reinvigorate me in you!

Bread of love, set me on fire with that love which annihilates in me what is mine and fills me with what is yours!

ASPIRATION: O Sacramental Jesus, transform me into yourself.

LITTLE WORK: Make a visit to the Blessed Sacrament to attest to your love for him.

Twenty-seventh Day
The Medicine of the Soul

THE SOUL: Even with so many means of sanctification and salvation, I recognize, unfortunately, that I am weak and empty. At the first occasions of sin I vacillate miserably and fall. Do I have recourse to Jesus in the Eucharist? But if my fall made me unworthy of him, that food of life becomes for me the condemnation to death!

Oh how good Jesus is! He has provided for my mortal infirmity and has given me the effective remedy to cleanse me from my iniquities: *holy Confession*. In the Eucharist he comes to me substantially, living and true, and makes himself my food and drink; in Confession he, instead, has himself represented by a man invested with his power so that I may have no reluctance to lay my abhorrent burden at his feet.

I kneel at the feet of that man, but it is always Jesus who receives me ... it is Jesus who makes himself my Redeemer anew, who appears to me in human vesture, who takes pity on my weaknesses, who counsels me, comforts me, helps me, heals me. I am not afraid of his presence, and even if I find it repugnant to speak to a mortal man, he changes my repugnance into expiation and fills me with secret consolation.

O Jesus, do not allow me to render so great a Sacrament vain! So many times I have gone to Confession almost by rote; perhaps I tried to minimize my faults; I found so many excuses to avoid humiliating myself for them! O Mary, Mother of grace and of mercy, accompany me to the feet of the priest and grant that I may emerge renewed by this Sacrament of spiritual resurrection.

ASPIRATION: O Jesus, give me the grace to confess well.

LITTLE WORK: Prod some soul whom you know to be in mortal sin to go to Confession.

Twenty-eighth Day
The Goodness of God in Forgiveness

MARY: Do you want to have an idea of the goodness of God and the hardness of creatures? Consider how God acts when he is offended and how men act! Oh how slight is human mercy, even non-existent! Man pretends to pardon, but in reality does nothing but treat his offender harshly while always remembering the offense. He forgives when he no longer feels the impact and the anger; he forgives with difficulty. Yet the offender is a being like him, perhaps better than him.

Look at how inflexible man is when he punishes: the guilty person repents, begs, weeps, but the law strikes him, obliterates him, deprives him of freedom and is not placated until he has paid in full.

God is infinite, he who offends him is a poor worm. The offense which he receives is incommensurable, yet God calls the sinner to his heart; he entices him with the most delicate expressions; he searches for him like a lost treasure, like a little lamb from his own fold, like a beloved son. If God wants him to confess his sin, it is for the benefit of the sinner, so that, by humiliating himself, he may feel free of his weight and deserve forgiveness and may look on this as a blessed right and not a humiliating concession.

God does not despise the sinner; he does not look on him with severity nor reprove him, but embraces him, enriches him with grace, reclothes him with the garments of justice, puts on the ring of sonship on his finger and prepares the solemn banquet of the Eucharist for him. One single sincere word of love, one single sigh of the soul is enough to reconcile him to God, even before mildly humbling himself before God's minister.

It is true that adversities befall sinners, but it is not God who wills the punishment and death of the wicked, it is rather the wicked who brings the adversities and disasters upon himself ... And even these serve God's purpose to call the sinner to himself when he doesn't listen to the voice of love. Oh how great is God's mercy! And you are still unsure about him? Do you not know that he considers himself greatly offended by lack of trust, precisely because he is infinite goodness? Throw yourself into his arms, then weep at his feet. In him you will always find the most tender and loving of fathers.

ASPIRATION: Forgive me, O Jesus, and have mercy on me in your great mercy.

LITTLE WORK: Forgive the one who has offended you so that God will forgive you in the same measure.

Twenty-ninth Day
Death

THE SOUL: I am full of life and it seems as if I will never have to die. Fantastic! I want earthly joys; however, without a doubt the day will also come for me when I will lie immobile and lifeless on my bed of pain and the scene of this world will forever disappear from me! ... A few days of illness will prepare my last day ... perhaps that day will also come upon me unexpectedly, maybe even violently ... I don't know. What I do know for certain is that this life will pass away and that I will find myself in the presence of God where I will give an account of everything, even of a vain or idle word!

What a terrible thing the moment of death will be for me: the body will weaken, oppressive anguish will take away my breath, memories of my life will assail me, the demon will assault me with great rage ...

O Mary, my mother, will you come close to my bed of pain? Will you soothe the terrible anguish of those moments? Oh, I await you because that hour will be too bitter for me when I remember nothing but the ingratitude and sins of my life!

The thought of death doesn't have to be fruitless for me now that I still have time and can prepare myself for it from now on. I want to detach myself from all that can cause me suffering in death; I want to renounce all vanities; I want to live in a Christian way in order to then have a treasure of merits. Help me, O Mary, to live well so that I will not then be oppressed by my great responsibility.

MARY: My child, remember that Jesus has given you a treasure that should serve you precisely at death and it is the Holy Viaticum and the Sacrament of the Anointing of the Sick. When you realize that your life is declining, claim this Sacrament for yourself because it is too easy for the false and cruel compassion of your family members to deprive you of it. Live every day, then, as if you were to die and measure your desires and vanities against this thought. In this way death will find you prepared and you will draw your last breath in the Heart of Jesus and in mine and you will be safe forever.

ASPIRATION: From eternal death, deliver me, O Lord.

LITTLE WORK: Say a prayer for the dying.

Thirtieth Day
The Presence of God

MARY: Wherever you turn, God sees you! Whether you ascend into the heavens, whether you sink into the abyss, God always sees you! He sees you, but his glance is infinite love because he is present to sustain your life, to help you, to fill you with the graces of which you yourself are not even aware.

God sees you; In fact, in him you are and you move. This is a great mercy. You ought to exult in the thought of being always in the presence of your God and in the meantime you forget it completely.

You not only forget him, but you live as if God did not exist. Even under his glance, with the strength which he gives you, with the freedom which he grants you, you offend him and you insult him! What an outrage and what black ingratitude!

God sees you and you ought to remember this in order to love him and to refer to his glory all that he grants you. You are his creature, his temple; you are like a living altar, and with what delicate reverence you ought to care for your spiritual cleanliness, the internal order of your soul, the blazing torch of your love which burns in the presence of God!

God sees you and what an ugly sight you present him of yourself! ... Oh, if you could see yourself as he sees you! ... You are like a house blackened with smoke, all full of soot, all full of debris and dirt ... And yet you know that God dwells in your heart! Get your house in order, live with the Eucharistic Jesus; live from him so that the glance of God is detained with delight on his divine Son!

You complain all too often that you are alone in the world and aspire to heaven! And yet you are not alone: God is around you, and within you, and living with you! Love him, then, with all your soul, with all your heart, with all your strength. Walk in his presence and be perfect; live before him with the trust of a son, with the simplicity of a small child.

ASPIRATION: I adore you, my God, here present, and I thank you that you look upon me with so much love.

LITTLE WORK: Resolutely eliminate from your soul, from your books, from your effects, all that could offend the gaze of God.

Thirty-first Day
The Offering of One's Heart to Mary

THE SOUL: O Mary, O my dear Mother, I've come to the end of your month and I feel a regret within my heart: during this time I've entrusted myself to you, and like a good mother, you have taken me by the hand and have taught me so many truths. Now that the month is at an end, it seems that I am now almost abandoned to myself. I am inexperienced, weak and forlorn; I always need you, my Mother, and, hence, I entrust and consecrate my heart to you.

Here it is; I place it in your hands; I entrust it to your mercy. Will you accept it, O good Mother? I give it to you without reserve, because I know that in giving it to you, I give it to God. You are the mediatrix between him and creatures; you are the advocate of poor sinners; you are our hope!

MARY: Come, my little child; I receive you and welcome you into my Heart. Here is your refuge, your peaceful shelter; I seal you in it ... come to me! This Heart of mine is the way to heaven; I make you pass through me in order to lead you one day into the bosom of God. Trust in me; be consoled! Your painful exile will pass and I myself will accompany you into the heavenly fatherland.

This month with me has ended, but not my love for you: I bless you.

Live in peace, in communion with the Eucharistic Jesus. Live a life of submission to the will of God, of prayer and of charity. Flee from sin; love virtue ... one day you will see me in heaven and all of your anxieties and your sufferings will end. Amen.

ASPIRATION: Sweet Heart of Mary, be my salvation.

LITTLE WORK: Spend this day in an act of unconditional trust in Mary.

Academy of the Immaculate Books Instruct, Inspire, Evangelize for the New Millennium

All Generations Shall Call Me Blessed *by Fr. Stefano Manelli, F.I.* A scholarly, easy to read book tracing Mary's role in the Old Testament through prophecies, figures, and symbols, to Mary's presence in the New Testament. A concise exposition which shows clearly Mary's place in the economy of Salvation.

Totus Tuus *by Msgr. Arthur Burton Calkins* provides a thorough examination of the Holy Father's thoughts on total consecration or entrustment to Our Lady based on the historic, theological and scriptural evidence. Vital in clearing away some misunderstandings about entrustment and consecration.

Jesus Our Eucharistic Love *by Fr. Stefano Manelli, F.I.* A treasure of Eucharistic devotional writings and examples from the saints showing their stirring Eucharistic love and devotion. A valuable aid for reading meditatively before the Blessed Sacrament.

Virgo Facta Ecclesia *by Franciscan Friars of the Immaculate* is made up of two parts: the first, a biography on St. Francis of Assisi; and the second part, on the Marian character of the Franciscan Order based on its long Marian tradition, from St. Francis to St. Maximilian Kolbe.

Not Made by Hands *by Thomas Sennott.* An excellent resource book covering the two most controversial images in existence: the Holy Image of Our Lady of Guadalupe on the tilma of Juan Diego and the Sacred Image of the Crucified on the Shroud of Turin, giving scientific evidence for their authenticity and exposing the fraudulent carbon 14 test.

For the Life of the World *by Jerzy Domanski, O.F.M. Conv.* The former international director of the Knights of the Immaculata and Guardian of the City of the Immaculate in Poland examines Fr. Kolbe's Eucharistic, spiritual life as a priest and adorer of the Eucharist, all in the context of his love for the Immaculate.

Padre Pio of Pietrelcina *by Fr. Stefano Manelli, F.I.* This 144 page popular life of Padre Pio is packed with details about his life, spirituality, and charisms, by one who knew the Padre intimately. The author turned to Padre Pio for guidance in establishing a new Community, the Franciscans of the Immaculate.

Come Follow Me *by Fr. Stefano Manelli, F.I.* A book directed to any young person contemplating a religious vocation. Informative, with many inspiring illustrations and words from the lives and writings of the saints on the challenging vocation of total dedication in the following of Christ and His Immaculate Mother through the three vows of religion.

Mary at the Foot of the Cross I *Acts of the International Symposium on Mary, Coredemeer, Mediatrix and Advocate.* This over 400 page book on a week-long symposium held in 2000 at Ratcliffe College in England, has a whole array of outstanding Mariologists from many parts of the world. To name a few: Bishop Paul Hnilica, Fr. Bertrand De Margerie, S.J., Dr. Mark Miravalle, Fr. Stefano Manelli, F.I., Fr. Aidan Nichols, O.P. , Msgr. Arthur Calkins, and Fr. Peter Fehlner, F.I., who was the moderator. Ask about books on similar symposiums from 2001-2005.

Do You Know Our Lady *by Rev. Mother Francesca Perillo, F.I.* This handy treatise (125 pages) covers the many rich references to Mary, as prefigured in the Old Testament women and prophecies, and as found in the New Testament from the Annunciation to Pentecost. Mary's role is seen ever beside her Divine Son, and the author shows how scripture supports Mary's role as Mediatrix of all Graces. Though it can be read with profit by scripture scholars, it is an easy read for everyone. Every Marian devotee should have a copy for quick reference.

SAINTS AND MARIAN SHRINE SERIES

Edited by Bro. Francis Mary, F.I.

A Handbook on Guadalupe This well researched book on Guadalupe contains 40 topical chapters by leading experts on Guadalupe with new insights and the latest scientific findings. A number of chapters deal with Our Lady's role as the patroness of the pro-life movement. Well illustrated.

St. Thérèse: Doctor of the Little Way A compendium of 32 chapters covering many unique facets about the latest Doctor of the Church by 23 authors including Fr. John Hardon, S.J., Msgr. Vernon Johnson, Sister Marie of the Trinity, O.C.D., Stephanè Piat. This different approach to St. Thérèse is well illustrated.

Marian Shrines of France The four major Marian shrines and apparitions of France during the 19th century: Our Lady at Rue du Bac, Paris (Miraculous Medal), La Salette, Lourdes and Pontmain show how, in the 19th century, Our Lady was checkmating our secular, godless 20th century; introducing the present Age of Mary. Well illustrated with many color pictures.

Padre Pio - The Wonder Worker The latest on this popular Saint of our times, including the two inspirational homilies given by Pope John Paul II during the beatification celebration in Rome. The first part of the book is a short biography. The second is on his spirituality, charisms, apostolate of the confessional, and his great works of charity.

Marian Shrines of Italy Another in the series of "Marian Saints and Shrines," with 36 pages of colorful illustrations of over thirty of the 1500 Marian shrines in Italy. The book covers that topic with an underlying theme of the intimate and vital relationship between Mary and the Church. This is especially apparent in Catholic Italy, where the center of the Catholic Faith is found.

To find all our book titles go to
AcademyoftheImmaculate.com

Please see the back page for further information,
ACADEMY OF THE IMMACULATE

About the Translator

Monsignor Arthur B. Calkins is a native of Erie, Pennsylvania, and was ordained a priest in 1970 for the Archdiocese of New Orleans. He is one of the most prominent among contemporary mariologists, having broad experience in both pastoral and scholarly work. His doctoral study, *Totus Tuus*: John Paul II's Program of Marian Consecration and Entrustment (New Bedford, MA: Academy of the Immaculate), has gone into three printings. His articles on Mariology and spirituality have appeared in both popular and scholarly publications as well as in the acts of congresses and symposia. He was named a corresponding member of the Pontifical International Marian Academy in 1985 and a corresponding member of the Pontifical Roman Theological Academy in 1995. He has been an official of the Pontifical Commission *"Ecclesia Dei"* since 1991 and was named a Chaplain of His Holiness with the title of Monsignor in 1997. Msgr. Calkins is the editor of *Totus Tuus*, the recently published anthology (in Italian) of the Marian texts of the late Pope John Paul II. This anthology was commissioned by the Archbishop of Bologna, Carlo Card. Caffarra.

Academy of the Immaculate

The Academy of the Immaculate, founded in 1992, is inspired by and based on a project of St. Maximilian Kolbe (never realized by the Saint because of his death by martyrdom at the age of 47, August 14, 1941). Among its goals, the Academy seeks to promote, at every level, the study of the Mystery of the Immaculate Conception and the universal maternal mediation of the Virgin Mother of God, and to sponsor publications and dissemination of the fruits of this research in every way possible.

The Academy of the Immaculate is a non-profit, religious-charitable organization of the Roman Catholic Church, a 501(c)(3), incorporated under the laws of the Commonwealth of Massachusetts, with its central office at Our Lady's Chapel, POB 3003, New Bedford, MA 02741.

Special rates are available with a 25% to 60% discount, depending on the number of copies of the same title. For ordering books and further information on rates to book stores, schools, and parishes contact:

Academy of the Immaculate
P.O. Box 3003, New Bedford, MA 02741
(888)90.MARIA [888.90.62742]
academy@marymediatrix.com.

Quotations on bulk rates by the box, shipped directly from the printery, contact:

Franciscans of the Immaculate
P.O. Box 3003, New Bedford, MA 02741
(508)996-8274
fi-academy@marymediatrix.com.

Facebook.com/*AcademyoftheImmaculate*
Online shopping: *AcademyoftheImmaculate.com* & at *Amazon.com*